FROM DREAMER TO CREATOR:
REFRAMING DETERRENTS IN OUR PATH

by
Karen M. Lowe

Dedication

To My Mommy:

Thank you for instilling the strength to

fight at a very young age.

Thank you for continuing the education

by living it out.

Thank you for the gift of education.

Thank you for the gift of YOU.

TABLE OF CONTENTS

Introduction

You have been dreaming about a venture, a trip or about achieving some other personal goal all your life. You have had this dream from the tender age of 5 and yet at the age of 40, it is still on your "to do" list. Three years later (now 43), you are at the first step of the startup phase of fulfilling your dream. At one time or another, from as young as when we were able to speak, some say from birth, all of us have been dreaming about that day when we will accomplish some dream; whether our 5th birthday party, our high school prom, our business career, etc. Since we are all dreamers by nature having a dream is normal, but pursuing the dream is the challenge. Also, we were taught indirectly to procrastinate (through actions) by all those older than us. We were constantly reminded that family comes before self and we have to choose one or the other. As a result, not following our dream, (i.e. not starting our business), keeping our hobby as just a hobby, is actually more common than chasing after it.

Is it any wonder that so few of us persist in holding on to our dream and creating it, while most of us put it off until 'tomorrow' when everything will line up perfectly? There may be many reasons why we wait. We may have been working on it slowly or we just procrastinate a lot. We may be very busy people with work and a family to provide for, which makes it hard to find the time to focus on our special dream. It could also be that we have little or no money to spare because of a low paying job with kids to support financially. We may continue to think about it and even tell ourselves that if we do nothing else, before we die we will start our company, or write that book, etc. The fact remains that unless we change the current conversation in our head and our environment around us, we will spend another thirty years waiting for the right opportunity to realize our dream. The disadvantage with the 'wait and see' type of thinking is that everything will never line up perfectly and as a result, tomorrow never comes.

This book that I have entitled From Dreamer to Creator is about how to change that conversation in your heads about fulfilling your dream(s). Rethinking how you see and think about, or perceive circumstances, calls for reframing your situations that prevent you from getting things done. This is not a book on planning, though you may be able to make plans as you read it. It is about helping you to look at the same scenario through different lenses, on a different level than you are accustomed to doing. This book will motivate you to follow whatever plans were or are already in place to create your business or any other project and if not, to use resources such as; time, support, money and a few others to achieve your goals.

From Dreamer to Creator will assist you in the process of moving your dream from a longing for something that does not yet exist, and help you in the investment of making it a reality. To invest means to make sacrifices, and my hope is that this book will make your sacrifices seem less daunting and that you will be strongly inclined to pursue your dreams. However, to be able to make the right plans you need to reframe the way you look at problems or issues. You need to convert them into opportunities and solutions. In this book I use the concepts 'reframe' and 'deterrents' instead of words like 'remove' and 'obstacles' because the issues we deal with are not things we can pick up and move aside. They include things like limited time and money which are real issues. Nevertheless, if you look at them from a different perspective you will be able to find solutions to create, in spite of the ever present existence of limited time and/or money.

When I started writing this book, I was concerned about my writing style. I was worried that readers would not be able to follow my thinking since I write the way I speak, which can be multi-dimensional at times. Questions such as: Would people understand my thinking? Is it too simplistic? Is it too complex? The truth is, if I followed my natural inclination, I would have continued to put off writing for the next three years, because of fear of what others may say. My sister encouraged me to write based on what I would want to read. She reminded me that there are people whose minds work like mine and they will understand what I am trying to say. "Let it be personal", she said, so that's what I decided to do. I reframed my thinking, not to focus on fear, but to focus on a selected group of people, something I should have been thinking about from the start. I am writing for a specific audience, and with that in mind, I have written this book using anecdotes. You will read about situations similar to yours from myself, clients, friends, and others about the lessons we learned through reframing. Also, you will read about how we reframed our experiences so we can build on them.

I did not start thinking about how long it took me to get to a comfortable place of entrepreneurship until I started talking to clients or potential clients. I heard a lot of reasons why some people did not start before, or why they cannot start, or why they started and stopped, or why they are unable to follow through even with coaching and supportive advice. The significant thing is that their situations are similar to where I am coming from and possibly where you are now. I entertained some of those reasons and excuses for not moving forward after I got my MBA. This got me thinking of how I worked through these issues and how I advise my client's to work through similar issues. I have outlined some familiar issues, then I offered reframing scenarios, and suggested solutions that worked for me and will work if you have the courage to try them. The biggest task that MUST be learnt and practice, no matter which of the multiple issues you identify with, is the willingness to REFRAME!

Let's get started.

PART 1

RESULTS OF NOT CREATING

Your Business Masterpiece needs a Cheerleader!

– Epigram Consulting Services

EVERYONE DREAMS

As normal human beings, at one time or another in our lives we all have dreams. Dreams may be defined in many different ways. They may be, "a sequence of sensations, images, thoughts etc. passing through a sleeping person's mind," or a fanciful vision of the conscious human mind; or fond hopes or aspirations that we all hope to accomplish." In this book a dream is understood as the latter. For example, a 5-year-old may dream about his/her first day at school, making new friends, etc. or a teenage boy may dream about joining the NFL or the NBA, or about a profitable career, while a teenage girl may dream of that special gown she would like to wear to her high school prom.

If we are privileged to attend college, we may dream about the job we are going into when we complete our academic program. At the job interview we may dream about the electronics or clothes we will buy with our first pay cheque. Parents may dream of the day when their young adult kids will leave home and their freedom from parental responsibilities, together with the joy of having a noise free house. Should I continue? Dreaming is in our DNA. Without dreams we have no hope, nothing to live for or look forward to. Dreams keep us hoping and hope gives us reasons for living. Some dreams are simpler than others and easy to achieve, but regardless of the simplicity or the complexity, they are all dreams.

If we all have dreams or hopes and aspirations, why do we sometimes struggle with what we want to do or pursue? If dreaming is in our DNA why is there a struggle to grasp the concept of dream realization? Why not push for what we already know we want? Some of our dreams are not career related, but it helps to recognize how natural dreaming is for us as human beings. When we become adults we start to struggle with realizing our dreams. Some of our dreams may not start at age 5 or 10, some could start at age 20 or at any age based on life's experiences, because we are all "born dreamers."

The question that begs an answer is; when do we stop being dreamers and begin to work on bringing our dreams to reality? Is there a specific time when we allow ourselves to convert our dreams into reality while struggling with life in the 'here and now'? Instead of turning our backs on our dreams is there a way to reframe how to achieve our dreams while living our current lifestyle? Another question to consider, 'Is it possible to live a fulfilled life without realized dreams? I will argue that the answer is no and yes. We are all different and so are our dreams. On the one hand, it may be that our dreams if realized could destroy us and others. On the other hand, our dreams if realized could fulfill our lives and others. It all depends on the negative or positive nature of our dreams. For the purpose of this book, we will focus on the positives.

Reader, may I ask, 'Are you in your dream job'? 'Are you in your dream life'? My cousin's dream as a little girl was to get married, have kids and be a nurse and she achieved her dream. For some readers, their dreams may be simple and easy to realize, but depending on life's struggles and circumstances it can be a mountain to get financial help to fulfill your dreams. Depending on the personality type your dream may be 'considered' more elaborate than my cousin's. What if your dream is to be a stay at home mom, but you cannot currently afford that lifestyle, how do you reframe and not give up this dream? If your dream was to be a CEO, but you are now forced to be a stay at home mom, how do you reframe your situation and not say 'life happens, move on!'

In some cultures, we are taught that a career has a particular look. We are taught that dancing or our love of history cannot become a career, they are not productive and cannot take us to the supermarket. We are taught that obligations trump dreams, and that dreams are a waste of time. I will propose that having all one's dreams unfulfilled is the worst way to live life. Some dreams, no matter how small, need to be realized, but with all the problems and difficulties some people have to overcome how do they fight to keep their dreams alive? In most cases, we subconsciously buy into the message that life is not a dream. For example, if you have serious entrepreneurial dreams or other positive aspirations and need to get to the next level, then reframing is a way to achieve this. Again, reframing helps to change our thinking and to come up with solutions to actualize our dreams.

One of my dreams has been to attain a

doctorate degree, PhD. I was once asked why, and I replied 'because I want to be called Doctor Karen M. Lowe, but I do not like to see blood. I went on to say it's a self-actualization thing. The person said to me, that's a waste of time and money. The little girl who dreamed of being a doctor is still in me, so I was deeply offended. My reply was, 'if you think self-actualization is a waste of time then you are going to be stuck right here.' I said that out of anger, but there is a lot of truth in that statement. Let's reframe this dream of mine. I just wanted to be called Doctor Karen M. Lowe, but if I pursue my dream to achieve a doctorate degree, based on our culture today, at the very least I can become a paid speaker. I would have needed to write a dissertation, this includes primary and secondary research and then have to defend my work to a panel of professors. People with whom I would have come into contact during this time would have remembered me, thought of me as an expert and either recommended me or asked me to speak at events.

I would have even been able to organize my own speaking events. I could have become a consultant and be an expert on topics based on my dissertation. Although, this dream has not yet become a reality, it is an inspiration because dreams always have alternate points of view. When I thought about getting my PhD it was not to become a professor and I did not even know such a position existed. After all, I was only 15 years old from deep rural Jamaica and already thinking about owning my company. I did not put it all together at the time, but reframing allowed me to see a lot more positives and encourages me to go for it.

What about the person making a lot of money and living comfortably financially? You have a six figure job, work 80-hour weeks, but you have little or no time for family and/or friends and feel unfulfilled. Is financial stability a good enough scenario to stop you from fulfilling your dreams? You are working three jobs to maintain your mortgage so giving up any of them is not an option. Is it even possible to reframe some scenarios to achieve your dreams? The issue is for you to decide whether the fulfilling of your dreams is more or less satisfying than your present situation.

Job Satisfaction vs Life Dissatisfaction

After majoring in business at high school, I studied computers for my undergraduate degree. Although I got high grades in school and graduated with a BA honours, I was not satisfied in any of my jobs working with computers. The money I earned was not enough to make me happy. I kept telling myself that living in misery is not an option, but for several years it never occurred to me that I was miserable because I had chosen the wrong profession, and to start working on the right one NOW was difficult. It is worth repeating that I was unhappy because I had chosen the wrong profession. I was not living out any of my dreams. I took jobs out of a necessity to meet my immediate needs. The problem with this is that I am a certified dreamer and I will argue that dreamers need their dreams actualized to feel alive. This is totally my idea, but I am sure a psychologist somewhere is trying to content my idea.

It was while I was in pursuit of my Masters in Business Administration (MBA) that I realized that I was doing what I truly loved. I was specializing in Entrepreneurial Studies doing courses like Project Management, Entrepreneurship and New Firm Creation, etc. I was doing case studies, working in groups, working on problems currently in the news and working with actual companies and I was thoroughly enjoying my work. I was satisfied that I had found what I wanted all along. Apparently, I can be a bit stubborn, because during my final year at university I was applying for corporate jobs. I had somehow convinced myself that my ideal job was in corporate Canada. Unfortunately, settling is far too normal for most of us. I did it briefly and it did not work out. Thank God for desperation for it saves dreams, because being desperate is what caused me to focus on being an entrepreneur, creating my own business, thus fulfilling my dream.

The thing about being unhappy with your job and going home to a family, or being with any other group of people, is that it permeates all areas of your life. You are now unhappy at home around your kids and family and this brings a further level of un-fulfillment. You are probably short with people at work and you start underperforming. If you are single your friends are now experiencing your unhappiness because misery loves company. Do you want to be an influential leader in a group of people who are all about gloom and doom? I believe not!

Therefore, when you find yourself in a

state of unhappiness and dissatisfaction, you tend to think about how this affects your loved ones and by nature we all tend to look for alternatives. If your child is unhappy you try to fix it; if your best friend has issues you provide solutions. In some of these cases, we subconsciously reframe the situation, we just do not call it reframing. The question to be asked is, what do we need to reframe? Notice I am not using the word change. Throughout this book we will talk about reframing.

Reframing is expressing or looking at a concept or plan or even a word from a different perspective. Another characteristic of reframing is repetition. When we are not in the habit of doing something a particular way, in order to get it as a part of your psychological self you need repetition and this book will have a lot of repetition. Here is an example of reframing, according to your schedule you have no time to spare, but here you are sitting in a doctor's office waiting. While waiting at the doctor's office you can get 20 minutes of administrative work done on your mobile device. In other words, you do have the time! You needed to see 20 minutes where it normally did not exist, that's reframing. Reframing allows you to create solutions that you would not normally see. Throughout this book we will be talking about issues that prevent us from fulfilling our dreams and will give suggestions on reframing them.

The 'All Who Feel' An' Nuh Get No Bat' Syndrome

Back in 2010 when I was working on building my experience portfolio and not working for financial compensation, I was asked several times by different persons if I was working. My answer was always "technically yes, I am just not getting paid yet." The comment that followed was usually, "how can you say you have a job if you are not getting paid?" I needed experience to acquire new clients, but for most persons I needed money to live and they could not see a connection between building a livelihood and simply living. The comment made me think of the "all who feel' an' nuh get no bat," song from my childhood. When I was young and growing up in Jamaica, during recess or break time at school we would play "bat and ball." This game is similar to North American baseball. Due to the fact that time is a limited commodity during school recess, there were always some kids who would play the field positions and not get to bat. This dilemma always created a problem among us kids. Everyone wanted to bat, as batting for all of us was the fun part of the game. So it would hurt when those who got to bat would sing and jeer at the fielders who did not bat with the song "all who feel' an' nuh get no bat go hide themselves in ah toilet…"

I feel like many of us are living this syndrome. We are afraid that we will play the game, put in the work and not get paid the rewards we desire. As a result of this fear, we are living unfulfilled lives. We are unhappy with our current situations, but until we decide to play the game, until we choose to embrace the boring and often hard parts of the field, we will not get to the fun part. We will not see the rewards we desire. This type of thinking needs a major reframe. You have to focus on the positives by believing and repeating to yourself "that next recess I will get to bat first or by having to field I honed my skills in 'patience' and focus since I had to focus on where the ball was going." Here is a good one for me, I even have time to study while waiting! I was forced to do a lot of research in the various aspects of my business. In working with these persons I learnt about the demographics and personality types I wanted to focus on and what I needed to offer and whether I was equipped to offer it. Each time I had to answer what I do was another opportunity to hone my elevator pitch and rework what I know or do not know because it was in these questions or times I recognized my shortcomings.

An acquaintance of mine started her own

business and did not make money the first two years of her venture. When she finally started making money, she was able to put down a sizeable deposit on a house and moved out of her parent's basement with her husband and children. Was playing the game of entrepreneurship a risk for her? Yes. Was not having a steady income for two years difficult? Yes. Was the payoff in the end worth the struggle? Yes, yes and again, yes. The rewards were reaped by her and her family in that she could comfortably make a deposit on a house and no longer had to live in her parent's basement. She was thinking about the future of her family and had to reframe her position in order to make the hard decisions. Reframing is the only way to hold on to our dreams, realize our dreams and still be practical in meeting our day to day obligations.

Part 2

DETERRENTS
OF CREATING

Find an area of an industry you love that is
not being serviced and create a Niche.

– Epigram Consulting Services

Interest, Or Lack Thereof

The first career dream I had was to become a flight attendant. I do not remember when it started, but all the way to grade 7 it is what I wanted to be. I was so into this career choice that my mom and other family members would refer to me as their flight attendant or miss world. When I was in grade 8 I had to do an assignment entitled "What I want to be when I grow up." The assignment included going to the airport to interview flight attendants. I stopped them, asked them what the job entails, what are the required qualifications, how they liked it, their best and worst moments and a few other questions. Guess what? At the end of the assignment I decided I was no longer interested in being a flight attendant. It was not for me, I felt the job would not be challenging enough. The only thing I remember about the job of a flight attendant is that when I was little I wanted to be one. I have never looked back at it and felt a sense of loss. I know this was a decision I made at age 13, but it was after research and a 13-year-old girl will tell you that she has feelings and is smart enough to know what she wants.

We must recognize that we have many dreams based on experiences and on information. We sometimes talk about our children in terms of nature vs nurture. Nature is innate, traits that we are born with like a certain personality type while nurture are the things we are taught, like being polite. Some of our career choices are based on nature, some on nurture and others are based on a combination of both. I do not know where or when I got it in my head that I wanted to be a flight attendant. As I said before, I grew up in a rural area in Jamaica. My mom did not have a lot of money so up to that time I had never been on an airplane, nor did I know any actual flight attendants at that point. For a while we did not have TV so I know it is not from nurture. It is not because someone told me to become a flight attendant. I am going to assume (because I really cannot remember) it was innate. At some point however, I lost interest! This, by the way, is not reframing. Reframing takes conscious effort and is not necessarily meant to change, but is meant to look at something with a different perspective. To see something for more or differently than what it was previously perceived.

There are many tasks to be done when you are starting up the pursuit of your dream to begin a business and still more to do once you get established. After you have established your first group of clients you may be able to outsource the task you do not like and have a hard time developing interest in. So let's talk about when you are starting up and cannot afford to outsource. For example, I hate accounting, but unfortunately it has to get done.

I started a company called Carys Belle a few years ago and because I hated accounting, I kept putting it off. I also hated administration so I put that off too. Here, I struggled with a lack of interest in specific tasks and not a lack of interest in the company or overall project like I did with being a flight attendant. There comes a time when I needed to decide on how many handbags I needed to order or what trade shows I needed to prepare for. I got stuck at this point because there were things that needed to get done before I could make these decisions. I had to organize the bills and other paperwork. Organize, meaning I needed to take them and other correspondences (those from UPS and potential suppliers) out of envelopes, put them along with invoices in chronological order, look at how much money I spent and what my revenues were, what worked and what did not work, put all my ad hoc notes and so much more together. I LOVE ideas, I love looking at the big picture, I love putting them together, I love research, I love brainstorming, I love planning and coordinating, but a lot of the other stuff, I had no interest in. At some point however, in order to be able to make this company work, I will need to reframe my 'I do not like accounting' attitude in order to achieve the bigger picture called 'my dreams.'

What happens when tasks are left unattended? They pile up! When tasks pile up I would sit at my desk and look at all that I needed to get done for hours. I had a hard time deciding where to start and I would take hours, sometimes days before I got up the nerves to tackle what is now a mountain. This may appear to others that I had no interest in my job (the big picture) but I loved Carys Belle. I loved where we were taking it, I loved the customers, I loved my staff and I loved the photo shoots. I just hated filing and I could not afford to hire an administrator. The problem is that the lack of interest in these small areas affected my ability to get the big picture done. It is easy to assume that I lacked interest in the big picture so I had to be careful not to confuse the two. A lot of entrepreneurs confuse the two and end up walking away from a dream. This is when a lack of understanding comes into play. Reframing is not needed for a lack of understanding, just the recognition of what the issues are, to be able to adapt reframing where necessary. In other words, you cannot reframe what you do not understand.

It is important to note that interest in a part of an operation is different from interest in the entire project. They are different and need to be handled differently. There will always be tasks in your business you do not like no matter what area of business you choose. There are parts of your day job (the one where you work for someone else) that you do not like, but you have to get done anyway. If you realize that the overall dream does not interest you after careful examination, move on to something else. Please do NOT reframe, move one! The quicker you examine the reasons for lost interest, the quicker you will be able to tackle your biggest and most important dream yet.

However, be careful of "losing interest" in your project. It is not a one size fits all. Examine it carefully for there is a difference between losing interest and being lazy. Being in a lazy mood for a month does not necessarily mean you have lost interest. If you have lost interest in something there is no way you are going to find the motivation to sustain it on a long term basis. Short term yes, but short term motivations does not build and sustain businesses on a long term basis. For this reason, it is important to examine your interests in the overall project to ensure it is still there. If your problem is laziness, then you need to find motivation and create solutions.

Reframing Fear

Fear is a killer of dreams. How does a person reframe fear, and is it even possible? I am afraid of failure, I am afraid of losing money, I am afraid that my family and friends have been lying to me and I am not as good as I think I am. After all, I do watch American Idol! The context of this book, and whatever you want to take away from reading it, is to help you understand that reframing is basically seeing an idea or situation in a different way than you normally would.

I have a fear of failing exams. By the way, it took me a while to be able to be this specific about this fear. I will start a business on a wing and a prayer and be excited about it, but no matter how much I study for an exam I am always scared to collect my results. I am sure psychologist have a name and a diagnosis for this mental condition, but my fear of failure seems to be limited to exams. Here is the contradiction in that: I have a MBA from one of the top business schools in Canada and I have never had to retake a course. I graduated with honours for my undergraduate degree and I never had to retake a course. I also have nine common entrance passes with grades 1 & 2. For those who are not from the Caribbean, it is high school exit exams and is required to get into university in the Caribbean and to get nine passes is actually quite brilliant. So where is this irrational thinking coming from? I study hard and I pass exams, what's the big deal?

It started with those nine common entrance

exams. Well I wrote nine of them initially, but only passed eight. Getting eight subjects is really good so that is still not a good reason. When I sat common entrance a pass was either a grade 1 or a grade 2. I failed English Language with a grade 3 (ironically a grade 3 is now a passing grade). If that was not bad enough, I passed Spanish with a grade 2. It is important to note that English is Jamaica's national language and not patois (our dialect) as most people believe. I am a naturally competitive person (participated in sports all the way past university) so to fail the national language and pass Spanish and English Literature was a huge blow to my self-esteem, especially since I did not believe in myself at the time.

The failing of English language followed me. What it also did for me however, was to push me to work harder. Instead of giving into the fear and not go for what I want (eventually I want my PhD) I studied twice as hard. I asked my professors for extra help when I did not understand what was being taught. I had a professor at Schulich who would say, see you next week. I went to his office every week for help. I reframed fear into 'you just need to work harder than everyone else', and that is what I did. After studying with my friends, I went home and studied again. My sisters think I am a nerd which I strongly disagree with. My reframing here is that I love learning and reading. I had something to reframe to.

I have accepted the fact that I hate exams and hate being tested and have reframed it to achieve success in school. Interestingly, I view interviews as being tested and absolutely hated them. So how do I reframe these? Become an entrepreneur. I would network a lot during and after my MBA. Networking was fun for me even though it was an informal type of interviewing or being tested. Potential clients or employers are checking me out and I am checking them out. Sometimes I did informational interviews with them where I initiated the meeting and I am picking their brains. At informational interviews, I am in charge, I am testing the other person. This led to a semi comfortable place when I go to their office for a formal interview. Being an entrepreneur, who is involved in a lot of networking, means meeting the right stakeholders to contribute to your business, whether clients or suppliers. In the process of networking, you are always selling yourself and your business so reframing networking to being a business task I love was an easy reach for me.

I have a client who was not performing what needed to get done and I tried every kind of pep talk and it would work for 5 minutes then nothing. Eventually, he said to me, the truth is I am scared and at the time his confession baffled me. In my mind, I was helping him by laying out a step by step process for him so there was no need to be scared. My unreasonable opinion is that there is technically no rationale for us to be scared or afraid, I believe it's a mind thing. Yet it is still there. Since it is not reasonable in the first place, finding a solution that does not include sitting on someone's office couch week after week for months or years is going to be challenging. Considering all the other issues that needs to be worked out it makes sense to just find a way to reframe it. For my client, his reframe meant not looking at the big picture. He had a business consultant that was helping him on a step by step basis so he could afford to let me focus on the big picture until he saw success which would allow him excitement which leads to a comfortable place to be able to look at the bigger picture.

What happens if you are not good or comfortable with networking? Find something in your business that you are passionate about, your number one fun thing to do in your various tasks. You are then going to talk about that task, but make it about the person you are networking with. Start by saying: "Hi my name is John and I am a business cheerleader or I make things out of wires (jewelry.) Try to use humour and allow an opening for you to discuss what you do some more. Ask questions to show interest in the other person as well. They may be your help financially or in other ways so focus on their role in your life and your role in theirs. 'What about you, what do you make?' You will find that you are both showing interest in each other. When I focus on the other person I tend to forget my fear because I am not thinking about me. I like helping people so my focus or reframe is that I will be able to help. In this you have reframed a situation and are no longer focused on your fear!

Money is Not Your Starting Point

Every business needs money to make it work. Until we go back to 100% barter system we need some money to make our dream become a reality. So yes, this is a big deal and a big deterrent in starting and growing your business.

For example, in my company, Carys Belle, I sell eco-friendly handbags. I started off with a manufacturer in Bangladesh. I did not know this manufacturer personally, I was not selling on their behalf and I did not have any credit. I needed to pay for the bags and the shipping (UPS, the transporter, is not a family member or friend's courier so I was required to pay.) I had to organize the marketing, the local bag tags and transcribe the information that was needed and I, Karen M. Lowe had only $155.00 in her bank account. I had no credit cards and could not get a loan from the bank. I had just left school so I had a mountain of student loans and had not worked in two years. I completed school during the recession and jobs were hard to find. The million-dollar question for me was, how do I reframe this problem?

This next scenario is not mine, but I know it intimately because I am the person's on again off again consultant. Let's call her Susan, she is a hustler, ambitious and talented, but money woes just would not stop following her. She started a dance studio and ended up being in debt and had to let it go even though she was really good at what she did. She did a couple of things in between including real estate, but again she needed to make money NOW to survive her now situation. She bought a camera and started doing photography with no experience in this field. Remember, she has a "no money" problem. If you think you have 'no money' problems, check out Susan. However, she is now a successful photographer entrepreneur. She takes beautiful pictures. I will talk solutions of Susan's problems in the last section of this book, but I need you to understand that what you are going through is not unique to you, others have similar stories and there is a way out if you reframe the problem.

I know that some of my clients are single parents and need to provide for one, two or three kids. This makes their situation seem worst because they have past the point of not having any money. Your scenario may be that even when you get money you cannot spend it on your passion or your hobby or any business for that matter. When money comes in, it needs to go to feed the kids, pay the rent or buy the children's clothing or pay for daycare. The question is, since money is such a big issue how do you get out of this cycle? How do you get to the point where money is not so tight? You have lots of options, some of which include either going back to school and getting a better job or becoming an entrepreneur. Depending on what country you live in and your obligations, going back to school may seem more daunting than entrepreneurship. Since this book is about fulfilling your dream in business I will focus on entrepreneurship as a viable alternative in ending this cycle that most of us find ourselves entrapped.

I will give some suggestions and scenarios in the final section of this book, but I do believe in the theory 'where there is a will, there is a way'. My motto has always been 'Money is not a reason for not doing something.' Start the process. The first, second, third or even the fourth tasks that needs to get done do not include money so just start, take your first step. This is the equivalent of taking one step at a time. Taking your first step and not knowing where the money for the business is coming from is more than reframing. It is the smart thing to do! But more than anything else, if you had the money some important tasks required to start your business may not get done which may cause you to stumble or pause anyway.

People tend to think of money early in the process of beginning a business because they tell themselves that if they do not have the money to make the business work everything else is a waste of time. They think doing research, talking to potential clients and other stakeholders is a waste of time. Let's see what reframing looks like here. Doing research and putting a plan in place before thinking about money is the smart thing to do. First, it is a learning exercise and gives you a big picture of what your business looks like. Also, because you really have no idea how much money you need until you have done the research to know the requirements for the business, worrying over money is pointless.

In lots of cases you do not know that certain things are required and the cost attached until after the process of carrying out the research and putting a plan in place. You cannot ask for money until you know how much is required so you really need to do the research and put a plan in place. Once you have done the research and put a plan in place you will be able to see different ways you can reduce the physical cost of doing business. Asking for money when you do not know how much is needed makes you look silly and reduces your chance of getting it. Remember, not having a plan in place will cost you more than having a plan. Conclusion, it is a waste of time and money (time and money you had to be creative to get) to think about money before researching and putting a plan in place.

Time Can Be Created

We have managed to convince ourselves that time is our biggest enemy for business or anything else for that matter. Most of my clients have full time jobs. Most potential clients have full time jobs and families and if that is not bad enough on their time, some are single parents. Some thoughts that plague your mind may include the following: I do not have time to live my dream; my children must come first; I will continue to work at McDonalds for minimum wage until

I can find something else. You will convince yourself that Time and Money are the two biggest deterrents of realizing your dream, but Time is easy to reframe. I repeat: Time is Easy to Reframe.

Throughout this book time is mentioned frequently, in several other chapters. Time is a deterrent not because we do not have it, but because we do not know how to maximize our time. I think we secretly like to use it as a reason for things not getting done. If we look at our lives we realize how much time we have and how much time we have wasted. In instances when I give my clients tasks and deadlines and tasks are not done, the number one reason for not completing the assignment (s) is always time. Truth be told, even when time is not the reason verbalized, time is still an indirect culprit. Time is relative. Whether or not we have the time is based on our perspective. Time can be created and carved out, but we need to reframe the way we see it otherwise; we will not take the time to develop what we need.

A client of mine, no matter how much he tried (his words,) he just could not find the time to consistently do what was required. If I called him and gave him the required cheerleading spiel he would do good for a while, then goes back to his old habits. The interesting thing about him was that if someone asked him to do some community work he was always available. If he is asked to work extra time at work, he is available. Even after he was out of work for a while he somehow still did not have time to work on his business even though he now had 50 to 60 extra hours per week. If I called him he would find the time, but just would not take the initiative to work on his own. His excuse was more often than not, no time. It is interesting to note that he talks with such passion about his dreams, his vison and his business. We did the whole self-examination thing and lack of interest was definitely not the problem, money was not the problem, distractions yes, but only because he was sometimes lazy and he also did not like some of the administrative tasks. Now that we know that time was not the problem we had to work on reframing his dislike of administrative tasks.

I sometimes wonder how it is that most persons who worked full time while studying for a degree found it so difficult to fulfill their dream after completing their studies at university. They finished studying which means they now have more time and still they tell themselves that they have no time. The key in lots of cases is recognizing that we have the time and that it is something else that is preventing us from getting the work done. At this point I encourage you to explore, why you want to start your business, and why you want to become an entrepreneur? Do you have it in you? Is this what you really love? Is this your dream? Sometimes keeping your skill or passion as a hobby is not the worst idea. Time is never the reason for not pursuing your dream.

SUPPORT COMES IN ALL SHAPES & SIZES

Lack of Support may appear hard to reframe and sometimes harder to overcome than other deterrents since this is about other persons and factors outside of ourselves. When we talk about lack of support, we tend to look first at our immediate family and that is not wrong, but we also need support from the wider community. After all, support equal sales.

We need support from friends, genuine support, not unhealthy support. A client of mine has been carrying on a business for more than ten years with a full time job. Sad to say he has friends who will use his services if he offers them for free or at a minimum cost. If they have a large budget they give their support to others. For the life of him he cannot understand why, since they will not tell him the why. This is not healthy support from friends. However, you can reframe this and use it to your advantage. In this case, their lack of support on big jobs, may be saying that they do not like my client's work. Instead of writing off these friends I advised him to reframe the relationship as a market research opportunity. Ascertain what it is about your work they are not willing to pay for and look at what they actually pay for at the higher cost.

Consider this interaction primary research. Primary research is different from internet research; internet research is secondary research. The positive here is that you sometimes need to pay for primary research, but with your unfaithful friends you can get it for free. Ask open ended questions as well as closed ended ones. I always have a differentiation session with my clients to see what they like, what they want their product or service to represent and which part of the market they want to penetrate. Do the same thing with your friends and a few from your community (focus group) to see what they are looking for. It is better to spend your time researching what market you want to play in and who are the persons willing to spend in this market, than to throw money at marketing and hope it works. Focusing on such projects will help you build a portfolio. The support or what appears to be a lack of support of your friends is important because this is where your marketing and marketing data starts. If they love your work, but will not buy your products or services, it could be either that they are not in your target market or they are your target market, but someone else is a better competitor to you.

Remember, if your friends will not support this project because they are not in your target market that's ok. This will help you to get closer to the characteristics of your target market. In this they have already helped you to see that they are not your target market. Advertising to persons not in your target market is a waste of time and money. If they are in your target market and will not support you, again, use them for research to see what they are looking for and what characteristic your product or service lacks. Information on your friends' likes and dislikes along with other research will help you to nail down a target market to focus your resources. Notice, we do not make enemies. We reframed! Instead of looking at your friends as being unsupportive, use their lack of interest as supporting your market data.

For those who will support you with cash, you now have the beginning of network marketing. These friends are the best first line of recommendations and sales. They will sell the product or service similar to how you would because they know the heart you poured into it. It will be a recommendation from the heart. When I sell my sister-in-law as a realtor, it is with an impassioned plea because I have seen her in action. I have spoken to her about what she does and how she does it and I see and hear her passion when she talks to me. When I talk about her work I understand her passion. I can say how knowledgeable she is, how she goes above and beyond and how she knows about ways to do things that are usually not advertised. I was introduced to someone who was moving to Canada and was dealing with a realtor who said she needed certain criteria. I remember saying to her: but Nic helped someone who was moving to Canada from England before they came here. I went on to say some of what Nic told me, enough to give more info than this person had, then encouraged this person to speak with Nic.

We need support from our community. This is where our marketing gets bigger. Your community is more than your 20 or 30 family and friends. Your community is an entire city, sometimes an entire country. When I launched Carys Belle we did it at my local church banquet hall after service one Sunday. My local church has more than 300 persons. A lot of them had no idea what I was doing until that moment. It was a blast, a success! It did not end there. My church is a member of a larger church network which allowed me to display Carys Belle at events put on by the larger church community.

I once read an article of two brothers who own a funeral parlor and instead of going to the same church they became members of two different congregations. All deaths from those churches go to their business and I am assuming the family of church members as well. That is community marketing at its best! What if you do not have a church? If you live in North America it is a community of immigrants. It has a lot of immigrant community organizations, join one.

There are lots of organizations that you can join and contribute to. Remind yourself that your business needs to give back to the community regardless of what you sell. Now is the time to find a way to give back. Still need help deciding? There are lots of "Meet Up" groups in and around your community. I doubt you will need to do this, but join a few Facebook groups and from them find local projects you can contribute to. I am a firm believer in giving back to the community. Long before I became an entrepreneur I was involved in community work, but later recognized that this is a great place to do marketing. If you are not involved in the community because of time or affiliation, it is time you reframe that thinking.

And finally, you need support from your family, and your spouse/partner. If your spouse is against your business something will fail, either your relationship or your business. This is where reframing becomes something else. You have to help someone else reframe his or her thinking. The bottom line is that your family and spouse need to get on board. I have been blessed that my family is and has always been supportive, but I know from clients and research that this is not always the case.

Some advantages you will enjoy when your family is supportive of your business ventures include; getting free labour, getting top of the line service, saving money and time etc. My brother is great with physics and engineering stuff. I had a hotel project once and needed to understand building requirements. I needed calculations to be done as well as a host of other information. He explained a lot of it to me as well as did the calculations. I would have had to hire an outside consultant to do this. My mom was my caterer at a company launch. I have brainstorming sessions with family members who are entrepreneurial. It is important to note that a mastermind group or advisors within your family is different from external advice. Getting your spouse to think you are the best chef is a compliment that encourages you to keep going. This is not always factual because of bias which means you need outside opinions as well to know who your buying audience will be, but home is a good place to start. My sister is constantly putting me on the defensive in asking me about business, but this helps me to be able to answer the hard questions when potential clients ask them of me. Looking from the outside in, you would think this sister is not on board, but I reframed the way she approaches advising me, she is playing the part of the potential client who needs proof that I can do the job. This is usually a practice session for me.

Now let's say you really are a gifted chef, but your family thinks you should keep it as a hobby and stick to you 9 to 5 job. They think your day job is what is best for the family in the long term. They expect you to 'suck it up', they believe that lots of people are unhappy in their jobs and working on a business on the side is a waste. You need to reframe it to your family. Correlate your business to whatever the needs of the family are. If the needs of the family are money and time, then show that there is an opportunity to make some extra income from this business. If the concern is security, again show them that you can lose your day job in the blink of an eye, but your business will be a backup. Another reframing angle is that this is an opportunity to teach the kids entrepreneurship and to do this project as a family. Another angle that we do not put enough importance on is what having your own business will do for you as a person. Explain that this will take away the stress of work from you and make you a better person to interact with all around.

INTERRUPTING FAMILY, WORK, COMMUNITY & READING

We all have them, family, work, community, activities, hobbies, etc. that interrupt the process of developing or creating our dreams. Here are some excuses that we make to ourselves; I'll just finish this book and read no more. I have evening classes. I need to be involved in this community thing, the kids have soccer and ballet. I have to attend my friends baby shower, I have an after work thing and I am too tired to do anything else. This report has to go in by midnight so I worked overtime, the 6th time this week. Yep, I work 6 days per week and I am so tired on Sunday I can only sleep and do house work but I'll start working on it next month. Where interruptions to our dreams are concerned we need to reframe them into something else.

There are so many things going on in our lives and the average person is not as organized as we may think. We do not even have the time to evaluate what is going on. How often do we remember a month later that this particular bill was not paid or an appointment was missed? A friend of mine actually forgot to go to court and ended up being found guilty because she was not there to defend herself. Parents have been known to forget their kids in a car, at a mall or at a friend's home. When I hear about stuff like these the first thought through my head is that they are irresponsible and need to be punished. Truth be told, they are not organized, but neither are we. We forget stuff all the time, we just happen to not do it in personal life or death scenarios. Instead, we do it in business life or death scenarios.

Everything in our lives is important and contributes to who we are. Our children are our life line, our heartbeats and they cannot do stuff for themselves. We need to do most things on their be-half. They need help with homework. They need our physical contact, to be their sounding board and com-fort. We are their taxi, their personal shopper, parent teacher meetings attendees, dinner provider, mommy or daddy sitting (parents do not babysit) and more. These 'duties' cannot be outsourced. Do you know what I realized recently? During our kids' time we have something that we would not normally have, we get more time. We spend hours per week simply wait-ing for our children. What do we do when we wait? Reframing what we do around our children will open up a world of opportunities we have previously ig-nored.

Our community is important to the

development of our world. We are all expected to impact our world in a small way to make the world better. Our community is our platform. It is in our community that people will listen to us. We have so much to offer and there are so many who need what we have. We may be volunteers at food banks or maybe we are activists for a cause or a local church group. Guess what our community converts to? Potential clients!

I once did a workshop for teenagers called 'Living Your Passion.' These were all potential clients if they decide to go into entrepreneurship. I also taught adults to read and write. One person I taught was a restaurant manager recently promoted and can no longer hide the fact that she is not able to read or write. If she decided to do her own business, guess what? I am there to offer my services. Your community service ties into your business plan, it is called marketing. As mentioned before, when I launched Carys Belle I did it at my local church. We did enough sales to pay for our marketing cost for that event and we had repeat customers and referrals. If we reframe our role in the community, we will actively work on our business while we are giving back to our community. Instead of seeing it as an interference to time spent on the business, we will look at it as working on the marketing side of the business.

Another interruption I want to address is family and friends. If your family is anything like mine, they are always there. Do you want to do this, do you want to go there, did you hear so and so, I need help and the list goes on and on. The thing with my family is that they are always there for me. When I need help and support their arms are wide open. What does that mean? They are staff! They can be delivery, packers, inventory, marketer, etc. At my launch my mom was my caterer, I did not know what was on the menu until the food came out. One birthday we went to dinner and on our way back we handed out flyers to business places in the area. I am also pitching my business ideas at family gathering. You have heard of a working lunch or dinner? Reframe every opportunity you can and call it working family time. Keep in mind that this lifestyle will not go on forever. Once you launch and start getting clients you will need to look elsewhere so your conversations will change. In other words, as soon as they get tired of you it is time to move on.

The biggest interruption to our business life can be work. If you work long hours, lots of overtime, you have a problem. Unfortunately, this is not a problem easily solved. I should insert here that entrepreneurship is not for everyone. After business school I encouraged a friend, who was having a hard time getting a job, to do entrepreneurship. She was honest with herself even though she was able to afford it financially. She said, at the time, it was not for her. A few years later, out of desperation she tried it, she failed. I mention entrepreneurship not being for everyone in order to point out that the only way you can work on being an entrepreneur and have a full time job is if entrepreneurship is who you are or want to be.

This is a hard interruption to reframe because you need your day job to survive until your business pays you enough to survive or you are sure your business will pay what your current job pays you or more. People have been known to stay miserable in a dead end job because they did not have the desire to reframe. Depending on what you are selling and the culture at your company your co-workers may become your clients. You can become a freelance consultant and sell your services to your boss. Reframe this to your boss as hiring you as a freelancer is a cheaper option, outsourcing, than keeping you on as full time staff. This way you can get a testimonial from your boss, a large established company, and take on other clients as well. If your business is food, offer to cater a company party or provide lunch to the business and co-workers. A photographer or designer can offer services to co-workers or the company's events. A friend of mine works at a company whose policy is to buy from its staff before external vendors. If your company does not allow any options for entrepreneurship, then find a way to carve out time away from work.

PART 3

RECOGNIZING DETERRENTS

Monetizing your passion is a good way to not give up when it gets hard.

– Epigram Consulting Services

Motivation vs Excitement

Some people are dreamers and will always be dreamers, no matter how much they try. As a result, they are not able or willing to work toward their dreams or to complete the realization of their dreams. The motivation or desire to fulfill their dreams has never been there, they enjoy looking at their dreams like movies and nothing more. If you are one of those persons acknowledge it and keep your day job. Many things motivate us. Conversely, we look at many things and for whatever reason we are not motivated by any of them.

As entrepreneurs, we need to be self-motivated. Even with all the external support needed to help us, we still need to be self-motivated. It is through self-motivation that we are able to inspire others to become our clients thus selling ourselves. When we are self- motivated it will show in our conversations. It will draw people to us. With motivation, we will find ourselves constantly looking for new ways to create our dreams.

At the beginning of most of your business ventures you are excited and you push a lot. This is not motivation but excitement. Excitement will push you to act, but excitement wanes when things get challenging, repetitive or boring. Excitement is important, but it cannot sustain a business venture in the long haul. In business, things very often do not go according to plans so being motivated enough to come up with solutions is important. This is where reframing your thinking is important. Recognize what excitement looks like and to be clear, if you are not excited about your venture, you should not start it. You will fail. Excitement comes from mentally seeing the product, the result and by telling yourself that success is within reach. You need the excitement to fuel the motivation, but the motivation is required to stay excited.

Motivation is the brawn in this duo while excitement is the heart. It is important to differentiate the two. Motivation allows you to create the picture of what the end product will create, after your research, plan, and hard work. Motivation is not research, motivation is not planning, motivation is not marketing. Motivation gives the mental fortitude to plan, to research, to implement and to not give up when things go wrong. The importance of motivation is that, it helps in the reframing so as to showcase the positive outcomes as much as possible.

It is believed that a dream can take you to the moon and back, but even having a dream is not enough to motivate a person. Dreams die more often than not because of a lack of motivation, not because of a lack of opportunities or lack of money. Entrepreneurship is hard and sometimes lonely. I once interviewed an entrepreneur whose products were in some major stores and while she was encouraging, she was also warning me of mistakes and expectations. One of the many things she said that resonated with me was that there will be months when, after paying staff there will be nothing left over to pay yourself. This conversation did not refer to events at the startup phase, it was several years in and she still had months when she had to be selfless. Motivation is needed at times like these. My sister is known to ask 'why am I working so hard and still have no money?' Yes!, Entrepreneurship can be a lot like that. Or the times when you do hundreds of cold calls or meeting after meeting and still no clients. Reframing your situation is the only solution.

The entrepreneur I mentioned earlier had a hat

business, she then ended up without a manufacturer. It took such a long time to get the first one that she decided not to find another manufacturer. She stayed in the fashion industry because that is what she knew, but she created a different product. She did not give up and the second product is performing better than the first. Motivation fueled her passion of being an entrepreneur.

I always encourage people to live their passion. Monetize their passion. One reason for this is, if you really love to knit and you are the type of person who can knit all day and things do not work out, at least you had fun knitting. Some people believe that not every passion can be monetized. I do not agree with them. I believe there is a space at the table for all. How you present your piece of the pie is what makes the difference. Not everyone likes vanilla ice-cream, some like French vanilla while others love chocolate and still others like cherry. You need to frame your product or service in such a way that it is different from your neighbor's. Starbucks is just a coffee shop. Compared to other coffee shops it is an expensive coffee shop, but Starbucks have managed to position themselves to be more than a coffee shop. Reframe your knitting, reframe your photography, reframe your consulting services. I am more than a business strategist, I am a cheerleader to my clients and I focus on individuals wanting to start their business or have been struggling with their business for a while. My clients are referrals because they experience my determination to see them succeed. I take on a client's project and own it because if they fail, I fail.

As human beings one of the things that makes us proud of ourselves is the fact that we are different, the knowledge that we are special. Knowing that we are different puts an extra pep in our step. You can reframe the purpose of your business to make you more motivated. Create something that differentiates your product in that it is working as a secondary purpose. We wanted Carys Belle to tell a story. Carys is Welsh for love and Belle is French for beautiful. Our slogan is to finish the sentence: My Carys Belle girl is… Whether or not you bought a bag we told you that you are loved and beautiful. Every time we talked about this product, there is a warm and fuzzy feeling for both sides, us and the person we are speaking with. This way, motivation is from different angles, not just from a need to make a bunch of money. In fact, if the only reason you become an entrepreneur is to make money you are setting yourself up for a rough ride. Make your mission about others, whether your family or your community. Reframe it to be much more than just a business.

Procrastination Is About A Tomorrow That Never Comes

Show me someone who does not procrastinate and I will show you someone who does not know the meaning of the word procrastinate. We were born procrastinating. Think about it, it took us nine months to come into this world. So for those who do not know the meaning it is to delay, put off doing something. I hate house work and I do not particularly like studying either. When I was doing my undergraduate degree I would find myself washing the bathroom to avoid studying, I had the cleanest bathroom in my neighbor-hood. What I never thought at the time was that my need to not fail was greater than my not wanting to study. I wasted so much time washing the bathroom and still had to study, it was ridiculous.

Why did I not like to study especially since I loved to read? It was a mental thing. I convinced myself that if it is hard work it is not fun. Also, the result, my degree, was too far in the future to use as motivation, or so I thought. I had to explore what was causing me to procrastinate, to come up with a solution. Procrastination in and of itself is not the problem. The problem is what causes you and I to procrastinate. Your procrastination affects all aspects of your life or your work. The workaholic is using work to procrastinate from something else, so being a workaholic does not mean you do not procrastinate. You can work hard at most aspects of the business but procrastinate from doing those three networking events per week that was included in the business plan. Guess what? Those three events per week is needed to get you actual clients and actual clients are what pays the bills.

We previously talked about a lack of interest as a deterrent. Similarly, procrastination needs examination. You need to examine your reasons for procrastinating which means, looking again to see how you feel about the idea, the dream or the project. I hate taxes so I leave doing the taxes as long as possible, usually until the last minute. Of course, there is a consequence. It piles up and I still must get it done, so examination of what the issues are early on is key to saving time. Referencing earlier chapters, if you are not interested in the project as a whole then it makes sense to stop and work on something that you are passionate about.

What about the thing you love; why do you love it? What do you not like vs what do you like about it and why. Knowing what you like about certain tasks will help you to reframe what you do not like into something you can appreciate. I do not like accounting even though math was one of my top subjects and love in high school. I started disliking excel because I now equate it to accounting. Lots of reframing, Whew! I am still not in love with accounting, but I am in love with financial projections so yes reframing, here I come. I have to do financial projections for myself and clients. I basically see financial projections as a picture of the business in the form of numbers and I love looking at pictures of the business. I love to have a layout of the business and a plan to work towards the layout. That's basically the backbone of my business. My accountant tells me that accounting is actually a financial picture of the business. I am still working on reframing a love of accounting, but having everything pile up too long is pushing me to keep a little abreast.

When we have no money we tend to procrastinate. We tell ourselves we will wait until we get the money, that's procrastination and procrastination is the result of a problem. The fix for this problem is to reframe because you do not have the money; you do not know how much money you need and will not be getting it until the time it is needed. Reframing is especially important here because it is hard to not think about money when you do not have it and you will end up in a circular argument which is unproductive. We talk more about money in the chapter Dreams Don't Cost a Thing. However, let me say here that reframing your thinking to tell yourself that money is not an issue will free you up to think up solutions. More importantly, if you think about money before you need to, you will get nothing done.

In most cases, when we start thinking about money we do not know how much we need so we make incorrect assumptions. We estimate higher amounts than is necessary and then bemoan that we do not know where the money is coming from. One way I deal with large targets is to reduce the targets to the smallest possible scenarios. I need to write a

20k words book, I need to write 2k words per day or I could break it down to hours. If I need to make $60k per year, I break that number down to the number of products to get this money, then a further breakdown of how many clients or sales per month needed and finally per week. This might look like five sales per week. It does not seem so big once I break it down. In this way I am not overwhelmed and it frees me up to do what is necessary to get those five sales.

If you think that procrastination is a character flaw and does not come from underlying issue, then how do you reframe? You keep telling yourself you will start tomorrow. you do not have a deadline, you just have to start and you will get to the next step. My suggestion is to begin by deciding on a start and end date. It is quite easy to procrastinate when there is no real plan. A plan gives you specific task and makes it look promising. There is a saying used often in Jamaica: "encouragement sweetens labour." When you see your potential on paper (your plan,) it makes you want to go on to the next step. Things start to look real and possible. There is a psychological thing that pushes us to work harder when we see results, ticking off milestones. It will help us to push through to the next milestone.

Another idea I will suggests is to change your deadlines. A friend was giving a speech once about being constantly late and that there was always a good reason, whether it was the traffic or a child got sick, all the reasons were valid. He suggested leaving an hour earlier, taking everything into consideration, all that will cause a person to be late. We all laughed. It was really good advice, but what was funny was that he needed to take his own advice since he was always late. What if we applied this thinking to our business? Set soft deadlines as well as hard deadlines. Focus more on the soft deadlines. We need a reframing of the value of time otherwise, like my friend, we will not take our own advice. We need to recognize the long term fallout of missing a soft deadline and have it at the forefront of our minds. We also need to look at the positives in sticking to the deadline and keep it at the forefront alongside the fallout.

Procrastination usually includes doing another task. What if you piggyback on the task you are using to procrastinate with? I mention every time I had to study I would clean the house. What if I listened to a lecture while I was cleaning? What if one of your procrastination task was to cook? What if you created some documentation while you cook? Speak into your smart device while you cook then use a converter app to convert it to words. I love doing research and one of my procrastination tasks is researching so I do research for my clients and my business. Find a way to convert your procrastination task into a positive.

Remember the name of the game is reframing. As far as possible, turn all negatives into positives and you would have succeeded.

LACK OF URGENCY TELLS A STORY

Why is there no urgency to your tasks? You say you are not procrastinating, so why is a 30-minute task taking you 3 weeks? You put in the bare minimum to get the work done. More than anything it screams 'this is not what I want to be doing.' You say that you are not procrastinating, but you are not working at your maximum limit either. It is now examination time. Be careful not to reframe the wrong thing. I try to work on myself a lot! I am always careful to be honest to myself. I will tell someone I am not in the mood while I tell myself I am being lazy! I will not necessarily do anything about it but at least I know where I stand.

Be honest in your self-examination. Again, if this is not what you want to be doing, move on! If this is where you want to be and you are excited and raring to go until it's time to sit down, then check yourself. Is it lack of knowledge? Could it be that you do not know what you should be doing? Lack of knowledge tends to cause us to drag our feet. When working with clients we look at where in the marketplace they want to play. What niche they want to occupy. This will be homework for them (and me) from me.

One client, who would not give me any information regarding what she had found, kept telling me she was working on it and she WAS working on it, but not getting the required information. The problem was, she had no idea what I was asking of her. When I say find out what people are looking for and what you want to offer, look online to see what type of fashion statement you want to make, I assumed this was a simple task. I realized, after the fact, that simple was not always the case. To put this scenario in context, I am not a photographer or a jewelry designer, but I need to know the industry of the client I am working with. I work with my clients on research, planning and building so that after our working relationship ends they are able to continue on their own. So, if I ask a client to research something I will do the same research in order to have a productive discussion. When the client and I sat down to discuss what she wanted I realized she had no idea what I had asked of her. She kept looking at stuff online but did not know what she was looking for so she kept looking and looking. She kept dragging her feet, with no urgency. It never occurred to her to tell me she was not sure what she was looking for. By the way, I have since fixed that problem; I am more specific in my conversations.

Once my client realized what I was asking for, her face lit up and she was way ahead in terms of possibilities.   Arm yourself with knowledge, seek help when necessary.   When your pride comes into play and prevents you from asking for help, reframe and remind yourself this is a teaching moment and you need to be taught.

A lack of urgency in your work could also be due to a lack of direction. If you do not have a plan you will not know where you are going. Unfortunately, most entrepreneurs do not have a plan. Have you ever had to go on a trip to someplace you have never been, having no friend or family at the desired destination? What are some of the preparations you had to make before leaving home? Did you buy a map or used the internet to get the directions? Did you book a hotel? Did you make sure that your car was tuned up or prepaid for an airline or bus ticket? Sometimes we neglect important steps like writing down the confirmation number, or picking up the driving directions from the printer. These are all factors of the planning process. All the above scenarios have a likeness to starting and running a company, but most of us do not think about it that way. In business we need a roadmap as well.

Being directionally challenged, a few of my experiences included stopping at the gas station to get directions. I encountered persons who could not understand the way I talked or who does not know the area. I end up going two miles or more out of my way or having to make long distance phone calls to get proper directions. All these mishaps cost money, whether it is to buy more gas or the extra time it takes to get to where I am going. Let's not forget, arriving at my destination late or losing an extra three hours of sightseeing or sleeping cost me money and a waste of time.

In our personal lives we do not always take the additional cost into consideration, but in business you must. It will eventually show up on your balance sheet. This is an example of going around in circles. You find yourself dragging your feet when you keep seeing the same signpost. At this point, you stop and create a plan. If you need reframing, remind yourself that there is a large cost and lost time attached to not planning. Remind yourself that time and money may be available, but still limited so they should be used wisely.

You will not always get it right but, planning will reduce the number of times you get it incorrect and help you to reduce the consequences of not getting it right. In writing a formal or informal business plan before spending a dime, you will see some of the flaws in your thinking and what you have neglected to think about. You will be better able to analyze how your idea will work. Writing a plan also means doing research. Primary and secondary research includes internet research as well as talking to leaders in your industry and potential clients. Potential clients will tell you what they need and why, while industry leaders will tell you their experiences, ups and downs, what was useful and what was not. Research gives a level of urgency when you have specific tasks and the understanding of those tasks. Reframing to think like a planner gives you the motivation and a high level of urgency in getting one task done so you can move on to the next thing.

PART 4

OVERCOMING DETERRENTS

Create a Vision for You and a Mission for your clients & Community.
Your Mission will allow your Vision to come to life.
– Epigram Consulting Services

I Dream In Colour

When I say I dream in colour it means my imagination goes into overdrive. I see myself in this beautiful light blue building. In addition to my office there are offices for directors, managers and business consultants all along the right wall. There are computers clacking away, there are customer service agents talking customers through the various processes or problems. There are graphic artists, web developers, writers and consultants working together to create. There is a brainstorming session going on in our conference room for the next video production, there are consultants walking through the offices on their way back from seeing clients and some on conference calls. I can tell you the consulting department is small, we have a policy to keep this department small because we do not want a cut throat environment found in other large consulting firms, we want it to be personal for our clients, the way we started. We have a research department that the consultants get their information from that allows them to focus on our clients.

There are six departments, Business Development, Customer Service, Film/Video Development, Mastermind, Consulting and Accounting. Our biggest department is our mastermind department because that is where most of our clients become self-sufficient and it is an opportunity for those with a small budget to get a great consulting program for little money. Our customer service department is huge and vibrant and loves our clients. We hire based on our clients' demographics to avoid language barriers and help clients to feel connected from a cultural perspective. We have happy employees which translate to happy clients.

I can tell you about the lunch rooms and the bathrooms and the boardrooms. We have two conference rooms that are booked back to back because we rely heavily on virtual meetings. I can go on and on about the infrastructure of my company, about our staffing and the role each staff will play and the departments. It's a large office, it's happy and appears to be a confusing office, but people know their roles.

Are you seeing the picture of what my company will be ten years down the road? I envision it and I picture it several times per week, sometimes daily. When I am at a bad place I go to my place of dream realized. I encourage clients to paint or draw a picture of their vision then hang it where they can see it on a regular basis. This way they simply look up from their desk and see it, especially when they want motivation or just to bring some excitement to their day.

A month into business school I read an article about big bonuses being paid to consultants. I cut out the article and placed it in my room above my bed where I could look at it quite often. I looked at it daily and anyone who came into my room would know what the article is about and what my dreams for post grad school were. I told myself this is what I was working towards. That all changed because I am my own consultant now, but it was a picture I could look forward to and it motivated me to do well. I adapted this to my current business practice and encourage my clients to do the same. It is a visual thing. You can see what you are working towards and it works!

If you say you have a dream but do not know what this dream looks like, how can you work towards it? If you cannot imagine what the outcome will be, you could be working on a failed idea. In encouraging clients to create a picture, I suggest they draw it themselves or hire someone to draw it for them. Put it on canvas or just a large picture in a frame or let it be your screen saver or place it on your wall and use it as motivation. There should always be a reminder as to what you are working towards. Notice I said working towards, not working for.

This is especially useful for those who have a busy lifestyle. It helps you to achieve perspective. Your kids are always in your face. As much this is apples and oranges, it is a good example to show how you are able to prioritize when something is always there. Your children will always be front and centre of your life but, if you were seeing your dream in more than your head and more than a fleeting idea, it would be right behind your family instead of behind the ten other things that will not bring you long term fulfillment as well as life changing results. Another argument in reframing the importance of your business could be that your business is your children's inheritance and yet you are wasting time by not putting enough importance on it. You might say you are single, my suggestion will be to examine your future, what is in it and what do you want it to be. A lot of us tell ourselves that we are not planners, but you make plans subconsciously. You plan or think about your trip next year, your child's education, your education or a funeral insurance so why not plan for your dream business? Recognize your planning habits and give your dream the same long term consideration and planning that you do everything else.

Desperation Saves Dreams

As much as I have had a dream of owning my business I have always been forced into going for it. I was not just trained in business; I have a master's degree in business with a specialty in entrepreneurial studies so why am I so intimate with the topic of desperation? Yes! I am a repeat desperation deviant/offender. I have been procrastinating for such a long time it became the norm. Then one day, I ran out of money, I lost my job (that I was miserable in anyway) and I am now one-month savings away from being a broke delinquent. Can I get this done in a month? I get through that period in my life and then went back to business school, earned my MBA in entrepreneurial studies and somehow ended up in another time in my life of being desperate with no money.

I asked myself, what if I find a way to feel desperate, before I am actually in the desperate situation. How do I do this without becoming unhealthy psychologically? Is this at all possible? One way to become desperate is by setting time lines. I have nine weeks to write this book. The first two weeks were spent on coming up with the problem I am going to solve and an outline. I set an 'internal' deadline of two weeks before the hard deadline for writing. I have two weeks for editing and graphics design as well as to formalize my title. I have two weeks to have external forces read and review and make necessary changes. I have a hard date for launch, but will bring it forward if the next two weeks are good. Remember, I am a procrastinator so on paper all that sounds great!

However, if I procrastinate there are several deadlines that will make me freak out. If I am not able to start writing because my layout is not finished I will freak out! I start feeling a little bit of desperation that I will not meet my deadline. I remind myself that if I miss my deadline I miss my launch date, if I miss my launch date I miss the Christmas rush and potentially the new year resolution crowd. Yes, even writing this line is making me freak out a bit. One missed deadline is now more than a missed deadline, it has a rippling effect on the various areas of my life and business.

I have had many opportunities in my life to be able to envision what I can potentially miss out on. I do not want to go back to a place of being broke so I work consistently on client acquisition even when I do not have space for one. Even though I have a picture of my dream I also have a vision and examples of what can potentially go wrong. I look at my dream several times per week, but I look at what can go wrong only when I have a project to complete. I own my dreams; I also own the potential to fail. Fulfilling my dream business is something that I feel. I am emotional about it and the thought of not getting it cuts deep. Sometimes for hours I daydream about it, look at the picture of it and have a connection. Having a connecting and thinking about losing something that is real will push me to feel a certain level of desperation before the desperate situation occurs. If this is not who you are right now, it means reframing.

Here is an interesting statistic: entrepreneurship rises when unemployment rises. It does not matter what country you live in; this is true because when people get desperate they hustle. If you are in your job and telling yourself that your job at this particular company, which you do not own, is secure then you need a major reframe! First reminder, if you are not interested in being an entrepreneur, then work on the next potential position. I was told by someone that you should always be looking for the next job. This does not mean to apply and accept a new job every week. This is done by constantly networking with potential employers and potential references. Potential references in that, if a position comes up, someone should remember what you do and that you seem to be good at your job and suggest that the employer invite you to apply for a job. This also means you need to talk about what you do and solutions to possible problems (in the news or from discussions) in your position as whoever you are.

If you are entrepreneurial in nature, then one option in case of unemployment is your own business. The next position you are networking for is CEO of your company. In other words, you would have been working on your business so the transition will be seamless. In this case, the networking you have been doing would be for potential clients, not for a job with another company.

Reframing the thinking 'I have more time' or 'I will do it tomorrow' will probably be hard after telling myself something for twenty years. Reframe means changing the way you perceive the conversation in your head. The conversation that is in your head needs to change. A new conversation could be: Fifteen years ago I fell in love with making bread. I told myself I would open a bakery one day. Wow, fifteen years lost out on an amazing opportunity. I am living outside of a forgotten dream and this is not good. Will I build the dream of this person who does not appreciate me for the rest of my life? I need to make some changes, better late than never. You need to look at what you have lost and become anxious, become desperate, and not want to keep waiting.

In business there are opportunity costs. The cost of the option not chosen when another option is chosen. What have you lost by not pursuing your dream ten or fifteen years ago? You may have given up financial freedom, more time with your family, job satisfaction or self-actualization. These are things to think about while you wait to fulfill your dream.

Dreams Don't Cost A Thing

You are now asking yourself if this girl is serious. Of course it will cost $40k to start your business. My question to you is: how do you know the cost of your dream? You have not done a plan to see what is required and the cost of each component. The dream itself does not cost a thing so let's rethink what you do first. Put the dream on paper. What is your vision? What is your mission? What is the reason for doing this? What are your objectives? Create a One-

Page Business Plan. You then need to research your industry and types of clients. You will need to know what type of market you want to get into. None of that requires cash, all you need is time.

You need to realize that without a plan you spend a lot more money than is required. I have done the math before a plan and after a plan, believe me when I say, you end up spending more than is necessary without a plan. Stop telling yourself it is boring. Instead, reframe your thoughts to say a plan is cheaper than jumping in without looking. Remind yourself that research is the equivalent of "look before you leap."

What is next on your to do list? Try something that does not cost money. This is an opportunity to test your idea. You normally cook dinner, arrange it nicely on a display plate, take some pictures of your dinner and send it out on social media. Since you have to go to this networking event at church, talk up your skills and give unsolicited advice while you are chit chatting. How about giving unsolicited advice to the guy who sells you sandwiches at work or that jewelry lady you bought your earrings from but does not even have a business card to hand out. Once your plan is in place you will become more excited about what you have to sell. You will find yourself talking about it to everyone you see and because you have a plan you are suddenly a better seller.

People buy excitement, if you are excited for your product others will want to share in this excitement. In some cases, you will hear, 'tell me more.' You are doing elevator pitches without even trying. This is where opportunities are created. Preparation meets 'opportunities.'

Now, think of all the options (even unlikely ones) where money can come from. When I started Carys Belle I convinced the manufacturer to sell me a small number of bags at a percentage of the overall cost of the bags. If it became a success, we would order a lot more. I convinced her to test her products in the marketplace at a cost to me. I convinced the agent at UPS on the phone to give me a discount and 30 days to pay after receiving my goods. I then spoke to a lot of my close family and friends about my idea and my dilemma and what I was thinking to do about solving it. An old family friend decided to gift me the cost for the bags and another gave me their credit card to use to pay UPS. The credit card was a loan since I had to pay it back, but keep in mind I did not qualify for a bank loan, but got a family loan instead. Here, my negotiating skills came into play. You can ask yourself, what skills do you have that you can use instead of money.

Above, I mentioned telling everyone about what I needed. You also have an opportunity (depending on your product or service) to do crowdfunding. Sell the product before they exist or take a deposit on services. There is the informal crowdfunding or the formal one like Kickstarter & Indiegogo. I am mentioning the formal ones because it is a good place to get market information as to whether or not your product is a good one. In order for formal crowdfunding to work, you will need a small marketing budget so keep this option in your back pocket for now.

For informal crowdfunding you may use word of mouth to presell to family and friends. In some cases, you can get a loan from the bank based on the fact that you already have customers. Notice that up to this point you have no need for spending your own money. This part may take three or more months depending on whether or not this is your full time job. By now, you would have gathered enough data to have a better idea as to how much money the business needs. Now that you know what you need you can now think about taking on investors or applying for community and government grants or loans.

During your networking, mention that you are looking for potential investors and grants. You can sell stocks for small or large amounts of monies. I once read a book where someone asked all her family and friends for between $100 & $500 and gave them stock certificates, a form of angel investing. This was easy because it was from friends and family. This particular idea is tricky and should be researched thoroughly. In fact, any option you choose financially should be researched properly to ensure it is the right option for you.

Barter some services but make sure you get as much value as possible. Do not do it if there is no value in it for you. The barter value should be of similar or equal value. Do not barter a $400 handbag for a $20 piece of cheese. A client/friend of mine told me she bartered her photography services for graphics and printing services. Form alliances that will allow you to know the giftings and quality of work for various persons and have them in your back pocket. You can use your alliances for network marketing. Market their products and they market yours. There are more grants now than before. Grants are based on age, where you live, social circumstances and more so check out options for community and government grants. Social media is a huge advertising platform and is free, all you need is time.

A note of caution: When you work with others make sure you set up contracts and be specific in laying out what role each person will play, what are the expectations and value of each person's skill set. This includes family and friends. I love my family to pieces and will go to the moon for them, they have been there for me in ways that I cannot imagine surviving without them, but this is good advice. You will thank me for this later.

Your 30-Minute Days

Here is an example of a work week:

1. Create & publish to social media

2. Research potential clients for cold calling

3. Work on Google Adwords

4. Work on website

5. Create Videos

6. Work on Webinar

7. Work on Business Plans (Make Up Artists & Catering Business)

This chapter is not about a work week. Instead, it is called a work *day*. Also, keep in mind that how you deal with these tasks depends on whether or not you have a full-time job. You may not have as many hours as someone who does this as their full-time job. I am a night owl, I will stay up late into the night, early morning unless 3:00am is still night; your sleeping habits will also influence your time.

I must give a shout out for Schulich School of Business, York University, because that is where I understood the art of scheduling. Business Consulting was not always my full-time job. When I was in business school I was involved in student leadership. At the time, it was important to get as much as possible from my MBA program and since I was not the party animal, I figured I might as well get to know as many persons as possible and be involved. I was Graduate Business Council (GBC) communications director, who had to oversee the publication of a yearly magazine, prepare a weekly newsletter to the school, attend GBC council meetings, take and distribute notes at our council meetings and meet with class communications rep and a few other activities, I called it my 6th class. This is in addition to carrying a full work load where each class involved group assignments. Business school is all about meetings, meetings and more meetings. When you can get away with procrastinating for individual assignments that is not an option for group assignments.

That sounds like a lot, right? There was also my community work. I worked with youths at my local church and we had international teen talent competition where I had to organize our kids for state and international level competitions. This job had me working with them sometimes four days per week. And just a heads up, teenagers are a handful. I also had a part time job on campus. I still made time for family and friends. I even did some small business coaching back then. I did not fail any of my courses. In fact, I did extra credits and to date those two years are still the best years of my life.

I must confess that before I started business school I had a lot more community work doing in my local church and wider community. Once I started school I dropped some of those responsibilities but did not want to stop all together. Community work kept me grounded so I made the sacrifice. I also mentioned in previous chapters other positives in being involved in the community. However, if you are able to give up something go for it. One thing I gave up, was the Peel Literacy Guild where I taught adults to read and write. Do not become stressed, as this is counterproductive to dream living.

Back to the issue of scheduling! When I started school someone showed me an excel sheet of a 24-hour 7-day time schedule on 30-minutes increments. It was the best gift ever given to me. Ok, the year my mom gave me a cross necklace for my birthday was nicer, but it was awesome. Once my schedule was created using this excel sheet, I sent it to group members to show my availability. Some of my time slots were non-negotiable to some persons. For example, Sundays were marked as unavailable until 11pm for all school groups and activities. During that time I was at church working with my youths and studying on the side. I always had text books or homework with me so I can do work on the go. I have been known to do homework on the Go bus. Thursdays I did zero GBC work. I did not check the email or attend meetings, this time was for studying. Remember, I spent a lot of money for business school so failing for me was not an option. I had to grab time when I could to do what I could.

If you have a full-time job, then your 8am – 5pm slots are unavailable. It currently pays the bills so that time slot is non-negotiable for your business. Working as a Business Strategist/Consultant means I use my mobile device often to get work done when I am on the road, then sync the data via online clouds like Dropbox or Box. I used Evernote to help me write this book between my computer and my mobile device. My mind is always working so notepad is needed to make notes as I go and excel and word are needed on my phone as well.

My job entails a lot of research so it is easy to do on the go. What about if you are a photographer? Photographers do more that take pictures. I have worked with them and they have lots of administrative work to get done and lots of editing. A lot of people in North America take public transit home or part of the way home use your mobiles to do some work. What about a jewelry designer? Same thing except, you can also design pieces. One young lady designed dance moves for my young people while on the bus. If it takes you 30 minutes to get home you have just done at least 40 minutes of work for the day, 20 minutes on your way in and 20 minutes on your way home. If you drive it is a little bit more complicated since driving and working is as dangerous as drinking and driving.

Try taking 30 minutes of your lunch to do some personal work. Set aside 30 minutes after work. Go to a coffee shop directly after work instead of going home. 30 minutes will eventually morph into 1-2 hours daily. I am not a morning person so getting up early will not work for my brain, but if it works for you get up an hour earlier than you normally would for work. Instead of achieving a project in 3 months it may take you nine, but the important thing is that it will get done.

A friend of mine wanted to do her degree part time while working full time. I kept encouraging her to start, but she kept saying she cannot imagine being in school for such a long time. About three years later she eventually started. One day after graduation she reminded me how she kept procrastinating and how she could have gotten her degree and the better job three years earlier. My point is, you will probably start your business at some point in the future. By not starting now you have lost money (opportunity cost) and it could also become harder and more expensive to achieve with cost of living going up. Still, who says you have to spend 8 hour days on your venture? If you really do not have eight hours, then use what you have. Use the 30 or 60 minutes each day and build slowly.

When I sat down to write this book I set a goal of two thousand words per day in order to achieve my overall goal of writing a 20k words book. Some days I wrote more and other days I wrote less. Do more work on the weekend than you do during the week (assuming you do not have a 6-day work week.) On my social media page, I recommend working 2 hours per day on your business if you have a full time job. What if you are a parent and need to take care of the kids? If you have older kids get them to work with you, use this opportunity to introduce them to entrepreneurship. Get your partner to help. If you have younger kids, while you are sitting with them, do some work. My 4 and 8-year-old nieces get bored with me after a short time. They just want to do their thing with me in the background. Bounce ideas off the kids. Yes, my nieces ask me intelligent questions that get me to think about what my next move in business could potentially be. Today, all of us watch a lot of television. Watch less television and use the time to do some work.

Once you have created that 24 hour excel sheet and you see the amount of time spent on "rubbish" or add up how many hours you can spend on your business for the year you are going to be pleasantly surprised. Taking a line from Scotia Bank "you have more time than you think."

LISTS CAN BE ALL THE RAGE
THESE DAYS

I was discussing my book idea with my sister and the process I took to make it seem easier than previously thought. Her comment was why did you have to be so technical, why not just sit down and write as you go. She went on to say she started her book a few years ago and she just wrote. I asked her if she had finished it. Her answer was no. My reply was, 'there you go.'

I researched how to write a book and a formula for organizing my thoughts. It included a layout and a timeline. I listened to and read what business writers had done before. Once I decided on the problem I would write on I did a preliminary layout by sections then went on to put chapter titles in. I then set timelines on how many words per chapter and per day based on the size of the book. I then wrote 2000+ words per day. This is a book based on my experiences so it was easier than say, a text book or even poetry but my plan worked. I did not write in order of the layout. I wrote according to the topic and what I was thinking at the time. I had to rearrange a few times, but it was still not as daunting as two years ago when I first discussed with someone that I will write a book. In fact, my sister said how can you write a book in such a short time when professional writers take years? My answer: I have lists. A list of topics, a to do list, a how to list.

I use a One Page Business Plan when working with my client's. It is a part of Epigram Consulting Services Success Roadmap program. Why? It has lists. It includes vision and mission statements, but it especially has a list of Objectives, a list of Strategies and a list of Plans. Plans have timelines that needs to be achieved. I tell my clients a One Page Business Plan is for themselves, to help them to be disciplined and grow, but they need the full plan for outside investments or loans. They are also able to build the full plan using the One Page Business Plan as a starting point.

Another question might be why not just let them do the full business plan. I have experience working without a business plan, even though courses I did during my days at business school included Business Plan Writing within New Firm Creation. I had the best intentions of doing it right but I did not. The prospect of doing a full business plan is daunting. Just the thought of how long it is going to take to research and get the correct data is encouraging procrastination. Most entrepreneurs do not have any sort of plan at all. Which is worst, a one-page business plan or no plan? Each of my clients did not have a written plan when we first started working together, and they are a mix of established and new entrepreneurs. As I mentioned before, my sister does not have a plan for her book which is still unfinished.

Lists help to bring direction and purpose to any plan. A one-page business plan gets to the point. It is not a substitution; it simply helps you to get to the next step. Think of it as a stepping stone because it contains a list of goals that needs to be achieved and another list of what needs to be done to get there. There are still lists that need to be done, to get the lists in these plans done, but you get the picture.

One of Epigram Consulting Services plan is to educate, so I need to post a certain number of social media posts per week. I create a list of what to do to get my social media out. I need to brainstorm and research what dreamers want to learn. I try to plan my week the Saturday prior to Sunday. I start my week on Monday with a list of to dos. Refer to my sample list in the Chapter 'My 30-Minute Days.

Having a full time job and or a family while trying to start and or build a business means not a lot of time. Imagine working on something then realizing there is something else that needed to get done and your time is limited. What would have happened if you had made a list of EVERYTHING that needed to get done, then prioritized the list. You then create another list for each item on the first list. This list then contains what is needed to get it done. That sentence just gave me a headache, but here's the thing, once you start creating lists, everything seems so simple. Let's say you need to fill an order for three handbags to be done for a client next month, also business taxes need to be filed, you need to cold call potential clients and create social media posts. The first, higher level, list would look like this:

1.   Fill Handbag Order

2.   Business Taxes

3.   Cold Call Clients

4.   Create Social Media Posts

Your second level list would look like this:

Fill Handbag Order:

1. Already discussed clients' tastes

2. Design bags

3. Confirm Designs with client

4. Create Patterns from designs

5. Buy fabric & accessories & thread

6. Cut fabric according to patterns

7. Sew bags

8. Ship bags (add timeline)

Business Taxes:

1. Find and organize invoices

2. Contact accountant to book date

3. Meet with Accountant

4. Call Revenue Canada

5. Pay Accountant

You then used my 24-hour 7-day week excel sheet (see chapter: My 30-Minute Days) and slot in the times for the different tasks and their deadlines. Finally, pat yourself on the back for being so organized.

Mastering Accountability With Mastermind, Friends & Me

This comes in many forms and what works for me may not work for you. Accountability may be from yourself, your family, friends, professionals or community groups. Holding yourself accountable is not as easy as it sounds. For example, my dreams motivates me to do more, and to stick to goals, but actually getting up and doing the task can be hard. I set my alarm for a 7:30am wake up because I want to get certain things done by noon but what actually happens is different. I finally manage to turn off my alarm at 8:30am, I will lay in bed and just stare into space for a while. From there I take my phone and read the news or social media stuff and if I am lucky, I finally get up at 9:30am; A far cry from waking up at 7:30am. I recognize my weakness to procrastinate, and one of my root cause is that I love to sleep. As a result, I put things in place to get me up like three alarms and people calling me. Eventually it gets easier and sometimes become the norm.

A side note here, as much as I love to sleep, I have been known to go without it when I need to in order to accomplish something. I once worked 48 hours using excel that had 20 books that interacted with each other in terms of, a simple update changes everything in the entire document. Additionally, each book had thousands of rows, and six years organized by month worth of columns. I use this example to explain that when you put your mind to something you can get it done. You just need to get the push to start.

One place to find accountability is your family. My sisters and my mom will call and say Karen, have you done 'this or that' yet? If I have something important that needs to get done early, my mom will call and talk to me until I wake up. My nieces are early risers so I need to get up early when they are around. Notice, I am speaking from a place of my weakness in that, I am not an early morning person. I go to bed late and will get a lot of work done between noon and 2am but some things need to get done before noon.

Setting a schedule and sticking to that schedule can help. Setting tasks to achieve your goals is another step towards self-accountability. However, setting the tasks and following through are two different things. The follow through happens because of accountability.

I had a 10am staff meeting every Monday morning to discuss staff requirements for the week and other deadlines as well as look at outstanding assignments and how to fix any outstanding issues. My staff is going to show up so I need to show up. What made me accountable in this case was my respect for other people's time. I hate being late, I believe being late is a form of disrespect to the other person's time, so I work at not doing it.

This leads me into accountability from self. Your thinking and principles will guide you to do the things you need to do when you need to do it. My job suits my not being a morning person. My 8 or 10 hour days does not need to start at 8am, I can start it at noon and still get my work in. I can book clients after the noon time and do my research at nights when all are asleep. Moreover, a lot of my clients only have time in the evenings to meet with me based on their full time jobs. Use what is within you and what works for you. Eventually getting up for my 9am meeting was easy, my body got used to it. I even went through a phase of getting up at 7:30am. That came from doing it long enough. Whenever I have early morning client meetings, I am on time because I need my clients to sustain my business.

A more organized way for accountability is Mastermind groups. I was doing research for a project I was working on and was surprised at how many entrepreneurs do not know what a Mastermind Group is. A mastermind group is basically a group of like-minded entrepreneurs (3-10 persons) who meet weekly or monthly to discuss and help each other's businesses. I like mastermind groups that do not all have the same professions. I find that a variety of professions bring original ideas because everyone has different issues and solutions that may be adapted to different industries, and make your company richer for the diversity and crossover of ideas.

A more traditional way is hiring a business consultant or coach. That's who I am so I know how hard it is for clients to get stuff done. I have clients that I have to give pep talks to on a weekly or monthly basis. The positive with consultants and coaches is that they have seen so many scenarios over the years, they are able to predict tendencies that can help you the client to be accountable or to avoid things considered the norm that does not work. By yourself, you are working in isolation. A consultant has used solutions with other clients and is aware of best practices. Also, it's the consultant's job! Accountability reframing is done by adapting a lot of the principles we spoke of earlier.

A FINAL THOUGHT

This is my first attempt at writing a book and what I ended up doing was putting a bunch of my thoughts on paper. Most of what I experienced, or that worked for others, may not work for you as is, but will work if tweaked to suit you. I heard a phrase recently that I am borrowing even without remembering the source, "there is a place for all of us at the table." If you want to become a millionaire, I am told you can, but it takes a lot of hard work. If you want to own your own little niche, you can and it too will take a lot of work but you will start enjoying your success earlier. You can work at your own pace; the important thing is to be true to yourself.

Reframing will not happen if you insist all your current deterrents does not exist. Recognizing that you are not doing all you can will work wonders for your dreams. Reframe the importance of realizing your dreams. If you think about it, your dreams actually change the world, one person at a time. You will create jobs through direct employees, this will change one or more lives depending on how many persons are in the household that paycheck belongs to. It will impact the lives of those creating the raw materials you buy in terms of financial impact. It will impact a community because you give back through your presence and service. You will impact your family in terms of financial stability and setting an example of going after your dreams and working hard. Your clients are being impacted by using your product or service. Remember Carys Belle? Our slogan makes people feel good just having a conversation. Fulfilling your dream is not just about you, it is also about your children and the rest of the world.

I thought writing this book would help not only others but myself as well. This book is meant to be a constant encouragement to change how we think about what has been construed as obstacles to achieving our dreams.

P.S. THANK YOU

If you have any type of relationship with me and you see yourself in this book know that:

1. You have influenced and motivated me to succeed.

2. If I have drawn from your experiences, think of it as a compliment to you.

3. It may not be your experience, but someone else who coincidentally has the same issues or ideas as you and I.

4. Start or continue to work on living your dreams, I am here to help!

A special thanks to Dr. Bernice Moreau for her friendship over the years that has allowed her to know who I am to be able to edit this book, and still allow my voice to be heard.

To my family and friends who have been a source of strength my entire life. Thanks for the advice, the editing, the encouragement throughout this writing journey.

To my readers, thank you for buying and reading this book. My hope is that you will gain a lot from this book and become a creator through reframing.

About the Author

Karen M. Lowe currently resides both in Canada and Jamaica. She completed her undergraduate degree in Computer Studies at the University of Technology, Jamaica and her MBA at the Schulich School of Business, York University in Toronto, Canada. This is Karen's first attempt at writing a book which has been one of her life's dreams so is now considered a creator. Karen is the founder and CEO of Epigram Consulting Services. Epigram Consulting works with entrepreneurs to either start their business or put a plan in place for development of existing businesses.

Karen is a proud aunt to 4 beautiful nieces and a handsome nephew. Karen is an avid reader and sports fan. She reads all books except horror and never reads the introduction until she had to do research for this book. Apologies to my fellow authors. Her favourite sports are athletics, tennis, cricket, football (soccer) and more recently formula 1 racing even though she plays none.

www.ingramcontent.com/pod-product-compliance
Lightning Source LLC
Chambersburg PA
CBHW061439180526
45170CB00004B/1480